Notes Relating to an Idea of Blue

Also by David H W Grubb

Fiction:

Beneath the Visiting Moon
The Almost Child
Sorry Days Are Over
Sanctuary
Fire Child
Hullabaloo and Secret Pianos *(short stories)*

Poetry — selected titles

The Burial Tree
And Suddenly This
From the White Room
Falconer
Last Days of the Eagle
Mornings of Snow
Figures and Masks
The Mind and Dying of Mr Punch
Replies For My Quaker Ancestors
A Banquet for Rousseau
The All Night Orchestra
The Rain Children
Turtle Mythologies
Dancing with Bruno
An Alphabet of Light
Conversations Before the End of Time
The Man Who Thought He Was
The Memory of Rooms (Selected Poems)
The Elephant in the Room
Out of the Marvellous
It Comes With a Bit of Song
The Man Who Spoke To Owls

As Editor:

The Gifted Child at School
An Idea of Bosnia
Sounding Heaven and Earth

Notes Relating
to an
Idea of Blue

DAVID H W GRUBB

Shearsman Books

Published in the United Kingdom in 2011 by
Shearsman Books Ltd
58 Velwell Road
Exeter EX4 4LD

www.shearsman.com

ISBN 978-1-84861-182-5
First Edition

Acknowledgements

Some of these poems previously appeared in the following:
*Poetry Review, Poetry and Audience, The Journal, Geometer, Scintilla, Smiths
Knoll, Sounding Heaven And Earth, Shearsman, Into The Further Reaches,
Sign, The North, Interpreter's House, Smoke, Ambit, Forum, Shadowtrain, Stride,
Bedford Open Competition, Poetry Salzburg Review, Essex Poetry Competition,
2010 (1st Prize)*

From Hepworth's Garden Out (ed. Rupert M Loydell, Shearsman Books, 2010)
Poetic Pilgrimages (Poetry Salzburg, 2011)

CONTENTS

for Beverly

PART 1

Notes Relating to an Idea of Blue

The man was actually seated away from the tourists. He was the last
to leave. It was then that I noticed his wine glass was full of stars.

I had spent all day in the field, away from the others. There was nothing
left to say and we would soon set off in totally different directions. Years
later he wrote about that day and how he loved.

The way that planes fly above our routines and tasks as if they were nearer
to something else. The silver of it. The density of it. All those prayers. All
those shoes.

The blue piano waits for Mister Punch. The faces of so many children.
Meanwhile Judy is having it away again.

Behind the stack of deckchairs the body of a dead hedgehog. It was
heading for another winter. Broken leg. Shoebox coffin. The small hole
filling with blue.

The lupin rising like a saxophone seeking jazz. The drowned boy,
always coming back for more of our noise.

The boy in the tree house saying "what we really need up here is a piano."

Reaching up in search of his father's letters he found a baby in the box.
The box was red; what an artist might call Russian Red.

We write these things down so that we might find meanings and
sometimes we do not tell anybody, especially those we love.

When the Hurdy Gurdy man departed some of us kept looking
at the place he had performed and the shadow that remained.

The Honky Tonk Angels and the Silences

This is really about an orchestra at night
and moments when you realise the room works best
when the river is sleeping and poetry invades the kitchen,
for we all love the men in red hats and yellow ties and what
it is to believe in clowns on horseback and the tricks that flash
and now honky tonk angels appear between the silences telling us
that every bird knows what it is about which is why their nests are
small blue boats that hide in our world until the eggs get up and fly.
I think I forgot to tell you about the man who draws on the walls as
he sleepwalks and when he wakes up everything has become blue; the pills,
the water in the jug as he takes the pills, the face of his wife as she
hands him the pills, the angel who keeps popping in to see if he's OK;
and then there were the blue horses in Ireland as they came into the yard
and moved out into the fields with the gorse jumping up and down
and those deserted cottages clinging to their beings in case some day sad
ancestors might return with the old songs and thin dreams and they
of course would be happy to share the stories of angels as well, the way
it was sometimes a voice only, a snippet of psalm or the sound of a bell
catching silver at midnight or a letter that suddenly jumped right into the
heart. I think I forgot to tell you also about Michael who now goes
out each night to plant the potatoes, kneeling down to place them one at
a time, no doubt whistling beneath the essential moon, covering them in
earth and words and his idea of Heaven. Finally, if it is the only thing I
do remember to tell you; it is said that when an angel has done whatever
the message is about there will be a pause and you will feel it raining at
the back of your head as if you had just been read by a brilliant poem.
Sometimes I like to think that ancient trees can see us as we gather in our
days and that the rooms in old houses are never empty and that a
woman who whistles does it to hide the memory of a man's obsession.
When we brought the dead horse down from the top field we had to use
ropes and the tractor and six men. We stood around drinking cold tea and
there were stories. And all the time I thought of the horse's head beneath the
sacking and the early morning light that was still inside it.
Much later we will come into our beginnings; grandmother smelling of
lavender, dog licks, father changing the subject, the god who does not love,
the gardener who takes his teeth out and drinks cold tea, dead birds and

dead babies, pathways in Cornwall that lead to nowhere, wind songs and
grass whispers, the meaning of the meanings, adults who never look you in
the yes as if you are untidy pets, shadow play and adult play and
the silences that appear to say everything and sentences that crack, snap;
the declensions of the dead, the husks of small histories, the ornaments
in the rooms as we move houses and pack what we want to remember,
and remember what we want to forget; faces, forgeries, forgivings. And
the silences of the eyes, the way a smiles slides across a face, the joke that
cannot have any meaning, the tick tock rescue of the clock or the watch,
these gestures of identity and secrets, these lonely and dead estates. Nettle
territory and wildness. Stone territory and wind jabber.
On cold days you can hear the silences, island moments, what we heard but
never said, entering spaces where the words were waiting, wanting.

When That the Sun

When that the sun has come up against the great unlit
and the teeth cleaning has become smiling and the school
has become its hum again and men have entered sheds to
hear the stories again and the women have spoken to bees
then what we know about battle and becoming and how to
milk and lay a hedge and the best way to approach miracle
has settled in the land and in the mind and in the meaning.

Then comes the bird song and what we do with hands and
the very old growing younger all the time and if the trees
are to fit in the living room where will the piano go for there
must be space for everything and the single shoe will never do
and the letters arrive from people we have never met smelling
of money and terror and the whatever makes the world go
and how would we like to live in a world without such nettles?

Then afternoon with its cradle voice and the quietness of birds
and always a man in the top field returning from a dead war
and the sun in the bucket like a big fish as the children come
home with dates and names and stories and the secret of the
meanings and we watch them in the trees and skipping talk
and telling us of people who can do jokes and visions and
did we know that every second of our lives was already dead?

Then comes the night with its closing verses and what we are
to do with dreams and the passages of prayers and those who
are to be bullied die all over again and those with bust loves
and there are always people who have been here before who
know why some animals will never return and that somewhere
there is a man writing the History Of Grass and when we are
sleeping they let the Rain Children in and listen to such quiets.

The Windows

We don't do trees anymore. We don't see angels skipping.
Jokes remain in their boxes and when somebody asks
what we are waiting for we say the silence of bells and
the poetry of ancient rivers.
The cat put itself out years ago and even the postman wears white
as he delivers other people's noises.
We don't do fields and when Mrs Webster comes to sing to us we
pull a sickie or pretend to sleep and Archie actually died as he
          pretended to.
Next month we are all moving to smaller rooms.
There will be rocking chairs of course and we will talk to our
mothers and fathers and lost uncles and remember the smell
of the children's bedroom and the roar of their dreams.
We will walk down to the sea and into empty classrooms
and see the cedar tree and the remains of the chain to the swing
and remember where we buried the dead goldfish
and the hedge with the dead tramp inside.
We don't do art and television and long walks.
What we do is rock a bit and recall interventions and attempt to
keep certain dreams at bay about betrayals and loss and poets
and remember birthday party laughter and the deaths of friends.
We don't do trees anymore; they have to get along without us.
Owls and red kites I expect and those white butterflies flitting
and the way light climbs down them until it reaches grass
and earth and robin soft.
We do gates though. We like the look of gates to take you off
and gather you up and when the next field appears there may be
people who will greet you with generous comments and plates of
sandwiches and jokes about what the living will do without you,
poor things.
Days stacked up like deckchairs.
We won't need days.
Next month we will all be doing future.
One day soon I would like to talk to you about selling
all of the windows.
Sometimes an idea is a pretty thing until we put it on.

You Will Never Be Allowed to Live in a Submarine

And therefore my friend you will never be allowed
to live in a submarine.
You can sit on an old tractor at midnight beneath the cracking
of stars with a silent friend.
You may hurl yourself into a wind and feel the whites of its mind.
You can visit the old peoples home when they throw a party when
another inmate escapes.
You may attempt to interpret what goes on in the minds of midnight
gardeners at the allotments.
You might observe the way that snow disguises the remains of the sniper's
secrets.
You will in due course learn that we all have silent songs
but, my friend, you will never be permitted to live in a submarine.
It is matter beyond wisdom and politics and what the world might mean.
It is a matter older than grass and mountains and oceans.
You are a wonder, a brilliance, a zazzle;
but, my friend, you will always be an owl.

How to Make a Horse

You will need moon and grass and the stench of nettles
and the voices of farmers and even their children
who have seen births and deaths and the way
men with ropes and small children
seek to witness the arrival
and what blood is about
and the manner of winds
and ancient rain
and the assisting grace
of those who have seen all this before
and their deliberate and cautious actions
as if their hands might at any moment
catch fire.

How to Make a Tree

Once there were dances and places where the sun
fell on the land as if planting a secret
and those who witnessed knew that
a tree was about future and nests and fruits and
the way sun might sing.

How to Make a God

A mountain can make you want to do this
or days when rain gets inside your sleep and relentless wind
and somewhere always there is a gate that should have been locked.

THE SPACES BETWEEN THE HEADS OF HORSES

for Clare and Emily

There were horses here once;
they owned the top field and when
they came down to the yard at evening
each one was heavy with light and grass.

At Easter, on the beach, they stood where the sea
became ice, stilled, hardly moving, as if they might be
searching for trees, hedges, a gate, that place where a
field becomes opening, track, passage.

Low light levels and shifting surfaces
and a boy with his red kite that must have seemed
like something on fire, jerking as if wanting
to escape, leaping to find wild.

But it did not happen; the kite was tamed,
dark sky appeared to suck away the sea;
the horses were led back to the farm
and a world of winds and water.

After; the horses were sold for slaughter,
the farm bent over, fell down, split, spilled;
I can still see the heads of those horses,
the spaces between when their names

were called.

Taking the Dead Horse Down

Taking the dead horse down from the field
late in the afternoon took six men and two boys
and bottles of cold tea and some more cake.

Most of the time we could hear bits of sky
still inside it and somebody said it was rivers
but I liked the idea of early morning sky.

It took ropes and chains and a cradle thing
and when it began to come on rain the horse
shone silver and smelt of old pear tree.

Dragging it across the yard the dogs yarled
and then one of the men got in the way of
the head as it swung down sudden; swearing.

The fact is its head was still full of morning.

When We Said Goodnight

When we said goodnight to the men on Ward Twelve
we sometimes wondered if they might be sane in their dreams,
the stumbling, worrying, collapsing ceasing.
Did they become earlier versions, bright and eloquent,
capable with shoelaces and door handles and crosswords
and getting the old jokes just right?
Did they get the order right, the sequences correct,
or even in dreams were they distant observers as if these dreams
belonged to other people? Were trees real?
Michael said he kept his dreams in a beautiful box
but now that he was dead there was no point in dreams.
Did I want to know?

Motorcycle

And when I was told that I was dead
I left the bed and walked out to the garden.

The owls were not there and the poppies
had completed their fire dancing.

I waited for you by the summer house
as another blue day became words

and then I went back and got on
with my death.

It was like eating rain at first and then
I met Chagall and he painted a motorcycle

which took us everywhere.

Because we were dead we could dance on
pin heads and sit inside rainbows
and enter poems before they were written.

I waited for you by the log pile
and knew each tree
that had been cut down

and then Chagall said he wanted
to play some more with the sound
of light.

Sometimes we played blue kazoos
and sat at the white piano with
Edward Elgar

who told us that when he was a piano tuner
everything in the world was possible
and that handstands were better than
bandstands.

I waited by the silver birch as it shed
some of its bark on the grass
like scrolls

and thought of what I might
write on some of them
to surprise you.

Life's Not Fair But My Knickers Are

—Fairtrade strapline at John Lewis

It's a good idea, like Braille rainbows and the parrot at
the barbers that keeps cutting in just when there might be
a silence or the Park Pretty sign at the side of the ruined hotel.
Even if you don't, we do, sometimes and often, I mean go there
alone, leave messages for people we will never see, salute Ben
Bloomer who is Head of Customer Services and who knows
what you eye you will one day buy. What you see is what you
dream etc etc. And there you go again, the eclectic tricking
the mundane, the dead angel abiding, the lost frozen in the future,
Jesus asleep in the park, somewhere a nowhere, ancient trees
hugging the future and church bells calling us to the always.
It's a good idea, like the poem that has no end and silent songs
and the snowman seated on the bench knows that there will never
be a snow woman or snow children or even a small snow dog.
What happens may never repeat itself, the farm in winter is about
arrivals and the bank manager got the job because his name is Jolly.
Then again, we keep meeting people coming back from where they
never left; Elgar's Dream Children hitting the hard stuff for all the
saddest reasons and the man from *Readers Digest* wafting jojoba.

SHOCKBOX, BALLYHOO AND GRASS BLOWING

I was nevertheless writing this late in the early
when the buttons were off and trash talk began
and there was again this dispute about just what
was who and did grass matter and whoever it was
who invented rain should remain locked in the ?
mark which was hovering again and I decided
to let it have its way concerning the life of pigs
and what trees see and what I might say in the
next sermon about the man not on the cross and
the trick of the tomb and what took place and then
there were boys in the field running down to the
stream to skinny dip it was so cold they must
have been ghosts of the Garland twins drowning
again at this time every year and never seen in
summer, in sunlight, in harvest time, in daylight
and sometimes you hear them say that the only
thing you remember for ever is the smell of grass.

New York, New York

The Ghosts of New York City

The ghosts of New York City arrive just as the entrances
to parks, hotels, art galleries and magnificent buildings close,
because America does not know what to do with its past,
it responds to memories of the future, the meaning of what may be,
the speeches that nobody has yet heard, untold articulations.
It is easier to deal with futures. Nobody knows. Abe Lincoln
becomes entertainment and there are few distinctions between
Ellis Island and Ghost Dances and Hart Crane and the silences of
a place like Cold Spring on the Hudson where you go to forget
and remember and hold close and drop and gather again and the
woman in the shop of delights is Welsh and wants to tell you about
the days when nobody arrives and how the past is present in the river;
and here too there are the ghosts that come into her shop and loiter
in the churchyard just up the hill and they get on the train with you
and they enter the city and they swarm wherever the living meet as
they love us, they want to nestle, they believe in what has been and that
everything will return and tell its story and demand attention and that
if the dead ever leave us the city will have no operas or prophecies.

The Blue Angels of Central Park

You don't need to see them; you just know.
You know when an early morning jogger
slips on absolutely nothing.
You know when the person in the pram
turns out to be an old man munching on a cigar.
You can tell when two cab drivers smile at each other
or when a single tree gets stuck in winter.
The blue angel is there when a poet approaches a rhyme
and when the President visits and has totally forgotten
that he has anything of beauty or truth or terror to say
and when the fat lady turns out to be Gertrude Stein

and she says she wants very much to see the Easter Parade
but first of all what have they done with her dog?
It is Good Friday. How good is that? Soon there will be
a small gathering of people who want to sing a hymn.
Actually it is an Easter carol and as ornate as a Fabergé egg.
The man who joins them has very carefully hidden his wings.

SNOWBALLING WITH FREDERICK SEIDEL

The yellow cabs now look like owls
in a movie about the end of beginnings.
In Central Park there is no centre because
there is nobody there but perhaps the ghost
of John Lennon and a poet who is very well
dressed and staring at the white sun and thinking
about snowballing in the mind. Years ago mean
boys stuck a stone in the centre of each snowball
and waited for cats who should have had spare
lives. And now it is this stillness, this withoutness,
this empty sky, these slow emotions of trees.
The game is up. The game is down. The yellow
cabs like fat old owls. Some of the windows with
the drapes still drawn as if something might happen.
The poet in the park, for example, who appears to be
collecting a store of poems to hurl at passers by;
red and dark green with secret centres.

Snowballing Without Sergei

We keep asking him. He would be very deliberate
fingering each snowball as if it might be a dead something
or suddenly aware that it might be a sacred thing belonging
to the sky. He would also stare and stare at the winter trees.

The trees stand like a series of exclamation marks and there
are places where the sun plunges through like a woman in a dark
red dress. Meanwhile we build a man with ice eyes.

If he were with us now Sergei might suddenly surge into action
insisting that the snowman should face the north
so that it would be the last person to see the sun.

As we walk past his house we hear the piano and there is
a snowman in the front garden and a snow child.

The Clowns of America

The clowns of America have given up tumbling,
mirrors and riddles, the laughter of God,
the way a day explains itself but does not explore,
the action that is no longer remarkable; there
are no more jigsaw moments to terrify them.
America is a perfect yard, a film about a film, a church
spilling out miles of smiles and even the ghosts get
rich, famous, invited back to guest shows longing for
shocks, the identification of fear, time spills and slick
soliloquies on stilts and the pure poetry of lies.
Each day they attempt new acts, inventions that will
crack the heart, stop the audience in its tracks, be seen
for seconds and believed for one day. And then they
wait to begin all over again. As if suicide were never
enough and drowning in the Hudson was a cliché and
what they wanted was the voice of a father in a barn or
a mother in a bedroom or a teacher in a classroom telling
them how to face the world; how to invent what you wanted
most and if you had to wear a mask make it unique and wait
for the day when you cannot take it off because it has grown
on you, it is your face and cannot be returned to the bag of tricks.

Birdland Jazz

The voices, the talk, the way the music walks
and the strutting recognitions and releases and
some of the women are so thin they would fit
inside a napkin ring;
and then this fellow appears out of the blue,
suddenly he is in the midst of things;

"I am Alpha and Omega he roars" before the big men
pick him up and lift him along and roll him out.
Four hours later he does it again only this time
he's changed his tune and the booze is ruining what
he wants to say which is "I have come out of light to
return you to wonder" before the big boys lift him high
and carry him stiff as a spook out into the blue night.

When we leave in the cab we can see him
walking on the river
shouting out strange things,
a ragged Lear,
and the hag by his side is Cordelia
only a bit bald and very drunk and slapping the old man
about the head and every time she hits him
stars rise out of his ears
and we wish him a long reign
and every thing but wealth.

Thunderstorm over Brooklyn Bridge

Hart Crane

And do we know what the memory is
the sad shadows of reflection
as the sunset cuts the contours
and we remember what we once said
about lives and tribes and the way a building
is more than passages and journey and what we
intend to become within the language itself is a
way of celebrating and lamenting and observing
the shades and shadows as if there was always an
angel just waiting outside our dreams to tell us things
outside our vocabulary where the poets eat and sleep
between their adventures, the ideas like tides taking them
across the harbour of dreams and skywriting and the way
that silences persist in the soul so that we may also discover.

Making a Meaning

In Central Park the trees are doing their flame throwing again
and the poets are thinking that this is what we need to do
to add adorations and meanings to fall; we die, we live,
we do dancing and discovery and death very well.
These decorations and silent explosions and the way the world
is transformed between trees and grass and climate and what
our watches tell us and these invasions of saints and darkness
and the woman with her unborn child making a mystery.
Here we go within the here we are and masks and tricks and
treats and when was it you last observed the stars and what
they might be about? The entire world is on the move, the zig
and zag of recognitions, the zither dream music, the way that
jazz coils making a meaning of our silences, the terror of
recognitions and that moment when a line from some poem
jumps up and the room that you sit in is suddenly strange
and everyone around you is speaking like birds and when
you look down onto the park there are poets and pranksters
and the yellow cabs processing like slick wizards and at
this time of year the ocean seems to come inland somehow
and there is that drift of whale song and the stars much closer
as we begin to send out signals and messages and preparations.

MEMORIES OF THOMAS MERTON

Very hard the words, the earth and light
coming out of them after days of rain
and doubt and nettles in the head.

Sometimes these silences are better
and closer to harmony and entering nests
of intuition small birds.

When there is no place for sleep
I keep thinking of the poorest people
and what they might make of stars

there being no place for them here but
barbed wire and chambers of hate
and the weight of loss

and how in some places their children
make kites to escape, to rise above,
to see what they might inherit.

KANSAS

The good people of Kansas come out of sleep
and wander into the banquet called breakfast
and the day calls and sun begins and birds.

The good people of Kansas do this because
there is no other way and God has made grass
and America is a kite that flies above the world.

The good people of Kansas are not afraid of work
and if somebody comes to the door it may well be
the boy Jesus who has a problem with a miracle;

and they will take him in and help him fix it and then
watch the story on television and read about it in the
evening news and never ever stop telling their friends;

until the next time somebody comes to their door with
a broken angel or a dead dog or a story about how their
baby has become a booby and surely $1,000 will fix it;

the sky becoming low and the rain always and didn't
they go to the same church years ago and what a mess
religion has become and even the trees acting strange.

The new billboard says IF YOU CAN — KANSAS CAN
and farmers still ride into the horizon but we never see
them return, their faces like old paper bags, full of empty.

LIVING IN SHORT FICTIONS

for Sharon Olds

Living in short fictions, slipping in and out
and the past just over there, quite loud,
you can hear what parents once said
and enter the secret rooms where speaking
to an imaginary friend often saved you
when you were not being beaten into retreat
with sweets, those instant songs, the way
attempts to heal were made attending to
the wrong wounds, each time the adult
hunching over your distress and telling
you about their own pain, their own fibs,
so that finally the entire house is filled with
people who have hurt and denied and got it
upside down and attempted to clown when
God was out shopping or the boy with the
huge head had been telling a lie when the bomb
dropped and he would never escape the crater.
Living in short fictions also means that silent
atrocities and private murders exist but we do
not see their filth and we walk past the same
ruined cottage on that same street corner for
years and never see the ghost coming in and out
and never find a reason to walk up to the thing
that was once a front door and stare past the
newspapers and boxes and stashed plastic
that are sunbaked against greening glass and
could that actually be a wig or a dead cat or the
head of something I think they called golliwog?
Different words, different meanings; what is said
and unsaid; the bits of fiction that never get said.

Illustrations of the Meaning of the Meadow

The only thing you have to fear is the man rushing towards you
with a dead owl in his hands,
the phone call from the publisher who says your novel is an opera,
the voice at the bottom of your mother's handbag,
the trick or treat boys beginning to spit rosehips,
the postman grinning as he hands you a letter postmarked 1932,
the boy in the classroom who says all Jews should live in zoos,
the snowman in August, the clockwork child, the blind mirror,
the photograph of James Dean as an old man in Central Park,
the closure of the very last bookshop, the foldover marriage,
the man who is rushing towards you with a dead owl in his hands
and wanting to know why you put him out to grass,
the small Guide To The Marriage Night in grandfather's desk,
the baby in the box at Grand Central Station,
hearing yourself saying the amens at your own funeral,
and the man who rushes towards you with thunder in his hair
and a sack of elvers who never speaks because of stones
and grass in his mouth so the owl speaks for him.

The Good Foxes of Night

When we have walked with the voices of our parents
and their terrible voices of adventure and truths,
the way the sea entered our dreams
and there were always the children who did not have games,
suppose there was more light than visions
and what they told us was haunted with loss,
my father with the falling fables
and mother instructing the servants how to pray
and every morning entering the chicken house
to see what the fox has done,
the nature of the violence and its rags
and then the story she would tell us composing
her quilt of seasons and reasons
and what it was all meant to mean
between the prayers and hymns and tiny screams.

The Blind Cyclist

Cycling into what he believes to be beneath sky,
between fields, what trees are, processions and the
tone of his friend's instructions as they are passed
by others who have no idea of what this means; what does
bell belong to, what is the shape of rain, umbrella, bridge?
How to see the being of the horse and understand why his friend
wants to describe pigs, farmyard, what the smell is and the sound
and the details about light as if everything depends on radiances
and why is it that shadows matter?

Sometimes the blindness has nothing to do because the movement
and energy and pace and sheer spirit becomes a flight, a flourish of
identities, the way of the voices, instructions, the noise of things
distant in the air and the way everything has a story calling, that
must be shared, hearing everything that has messages and wings.
What is kite? What is cloud formation? What is flag of Saint George?
A gate is not a place, is between things, it either side, inside and out.
A window cannot speak. Is an angel a window, seeing right through
the invisible truths that I can hold and become and fully understand?

Rain wipes. Wind is skipping.
I am seven. What is shadow?
I can do light. Bird babble.
What a window sees.
What a door says.
The gate into the field into the sun.
Do pigs have smiles?
Sometimes the blindness has nothing to do.
I can do amazing.

MISTER HUDSON AND THE WORLD

Mister Hudson expects the world to come to him;
voices, headlines, waiting for the Cutters to extract
something juicy, mostly bouncing along with the banal,
the ways we are, leaving shock and wisdom to others
and the weather hauled forth as if our lives depended.
The Cutters know what we want, the tip will tell them
and Mister Hudson from his vantage point never lets on.
That older man, look at him now as she tells him she
comes from Hungary and would he like his ears done?
He wonders whether they might talk about the Uprising
or about how she came to England as she lifts his left
lobe to remove three hairs that his wife once dealt with.
Mister Hudson knows that he is also thinking about the
appropriate tip and whether generosity will be mistaken.
During a typical day the newspapers will get mauled, the
large white bag of hair will be filled three times, they will
walk away looking at themselves in case something is not
quite as it might be. A few say cheerio to Mister Hudson
as if he might retort with a splash of sound, raise a laugh,
zap the moment but it never happens. At five thirty he enters
his cage again, preens, struts his stuff and waits for the glow.
He dreams of the backs of their heads; pretty girls, the way
they lean in and out, the flow of light, amazing azure tilts.

WALKING INTO WILD

It began with a length of hose, safe to the ground;
then string, rope, pole, wire, the dare to be above what
the rest of us might be about and our need for fantasy
and standing in the sky and the realms of disorder and dare;

and it made him famous in the circus, the showground,
the cavern and the gorge, making ladders in the sky and
crossing between certainty and dream and the repeats
of the explicit and conditions and what we knew was true;

but what we did not see was his moonwalking, alone,
when we were all asleep and screwed into dreams and
the light looked the other way and the moon was blind
and even the cats had given up their satires and soliloquies;

off the ledge of his house, towards whatever there was
of star squint and moon hue and the distant aircraft that
flew to routine and order and the scheduled and purchased,
walking so far as the rope went and then walking some more.

This way he defeated the arranged, the rehearsed, the way
we make things happen; this way he denied the motivational
and all that the media might say, this way he derided stunt and
kept going, kept pretending, heading for the unknown equations.

And did he want to be seen, did he expect a lover to shout out
something about forgiveness and restoration, did he hope that
somebody in silver would arrive and take his number and
suggest that there were forms to be filled in and that there
was no room for this sort of antic, madness, walking into wild?

TIGER TRYST

And it is a green tiger
who lies down beside those who are already lost

to be with whatever idea remains with them
and the fall of their music that never departs.

And it is a white tiger
who looks out for our children as they discover light

and what it is that music does
and the humming of rain and the slap of sudden silence.

And it a red tiger
who roams between the old men playing cards and women

who knit garments for sons who will never return
from vanishing and earth sermons and the rip of fear.

And it is the black tiger
rippling through night grass, a secret gleam

that nobody mentions in case the stars dissolve and moon
maddens the horses and snakes begin to speak again.

And it is a red tiger,
its cut and flash and eyes like wounds

that the poets speak of sometimes
and the holy men seek to deny.

THE DYING HOUSE

First to go are the words,
out the doors with the last people,
out into other days and places and
whatever makes their lives work
which may be exactly the same
but in another colour and hue
and of course also the dreams
as if they had entered another
set of songs, as if the garden
had changed its dress or a child
stopped in the middle of a song
because the song had found other.

Perhaps the reason for leaving
had been concise and clear and
although the final hours may
have been a mystery because
the men found the piano heavy
or the blankets didn't entirely
keep out the rain or a child
refused to leave a tree house
or trouble with keys or one
of them had started to take out
the lightbulbs or even a brass
dream or the memory of lies

or the view across the garden
to hills that suddenly were white
then golden then green again as
if the view could be music and then
for a few seconds standing where
the deathbed had been removed
and the carpet was now pierced
deep with a stain and some words
were still hiding, still holding on
about the reason for leaving and

what the child had said and the way
the doctor suddenly ran out of words.

OF MICE AND MEN AND THEN

For the rest of our lives we are left with what
we have to do when nobody else is going to do it for us.
We can call this endings or shut downs or endtimes
or where was God? or walking into the distance.
This is done in opera and film and strange poems
and photographs and dream scenes but mostly inside our souls
and in prayers and when there is that feeling that the last mile
has been walked and the last speech made and the distance is there
a few feet in front of us. Scott thinking of his family and Saint Francis
when the light has gone and each person as they are hurled towards outer
space and are whited out. Sudden. The poet Clare clawing his way back to
fields of light and Beethoven rocking in the silence of his own notations.
The snow silence. The earth not hearing.
The careless stars. The light that is trapped in a darkness.
The idea that is called madness. Earth whisper and stone silence
and the relentless persuasions and skinned epiphanies.
The discovery of a love letter that you never posted.

SHADOW PLAY

What do you want this to be, in the memory,
in the heart? The way things were said, the silences saying,
the handshake, the way the words ran out, those who were there
and the feelings that this has taken place before and we are within
mosaics of music and cadences and trust?
What you see is what you don't say, what you remember is what
love said, what eclipsed, something clutched between murder and trust
and the way the world looked away, the way truths gets trampled and
we love our fathers and every so often all the clocks in the world
have stopped, the soliloquies stunted, the moonrise unique, a child
running across a field and the thousands of days between.

Vanishing

Spreadeagled sunlight at the centre of the field;
a smashed tractor submerged where there had been
badgers; nettles, withers of white grass, strewn rags
and rabbit crap where the wind was always cornered.

And there they are again, the four boys, one of them
undressing, two as if on guard and the one who never
stops talking to the naked boy who is going to turn
himself inside out, from head to toe, and then return.

He has to keep talking to tell him what it looks like
from the outside of the inside out, speaking to where
the ears should be, making sure that the boy knows all
the time what state he has become in his undressing;

so that he knows when to stop, and begin to return, and
not get lost within the bone and strain of it, the other being,
the animal state, its blindness and necessities, its being beyond;
so that he can reverse what he has done and become the boy

again; the boy in the field in the sun again; the lookout boys
relaxing now and the one who did all the talking silenced by
marvel and wonder, the secret trick, the risk of it, forgetting
the man who told them how to do it, his yarn, his vanishing.

THE GRASS GOD

i.m. James Turner

Once we saw him, the Grass God;
after the shine of rain had gone away
the skin of the sky was low where there
had been stars and the sea wind turned
in its early morning tides, the lichen on
the wall like dead fish eyes and the bell
from Saint Minver hooded, as if a secret
was being told, a Cornish secret, sudden
and ancient, coming back to bite so that
we might remember something; and then
we saw the Grass God, the shimmer, the
light that was hollow, folding and bending,
breaking blue and green and silver, racing
ahead of us, beside and behind, catching
in and out, to remind us of what was once
here, the truth and the trick of it, the meaning
and the mercy of it, then the light lifting him
across the dunes and the bay suddenly dark;
the sun had run away and we were left cold
in steel silence, the bell of Saint Minver stalled;
and in the barn we waited for the ordinary to
return, the collapse of the miraculous, an end
to angels, the sound of a tractor, gulls yawping.

ICE

Not the men spitting snow, not the earth like black rope,
not the dead rat stuck in a sack of stench;
not the glass yard and the tree that had burst above us;
not the silence of birds and the wind like wire and each
morning dragging us from sleep towards the slow motion
horses heads hanging low and the byre tight with silence and
the windows filled with white fear faces and the child in
the top room fever singing; none of this did for us until at the
door stood the man in rags, his eyes of stone, and the woman
with thorns in her face telling us that they had come from a
nowhere and nothing land and could we give them sleep and
cake and did we know of another home that might hide them?
All night moon tides and other voices and when we awoke
they had gone and the slipping sun was gristle and our sons
went into the yard and came back swearing and spitting shit;
gobbing their food and telling us what they found dead in
the top shed; she with nails in her face and the man stripped
naked, wanting it finished, nothing left, his torso twisted turnip.
It will take sacking and rope to get them out of there, bundled
like creatures in some ancient saga, ice bound into green sea.

LOOKING AFTER MY FATHER

No; I am not free to meet you today,
I am looking after my father.
The trees will have to wait for there are
things that must be done
and I am looking after my father.
There are matters that must be dealt with
and versions to be clarified
and I am looking after my father.
There are fields that must be visited
and stories that I have to listen to
and I am looking after my father.
Some of the moments are still broken
and the sound of distances comes nearer
and what is future needs to be assembled and
there are images to be put in new places and
some of the seconds have become entire days
and I am looking after my father although it is
true that he died so many years ago; his noise.

THE SECRET SQUIRREL

The squirrel will be in the Teletower at midnight
and there will be arrangements,
meanwhile look out for the man who eats his hat
at Café du Lac because he is an imposter
and keep your mind on other things
such as the angels they dug up in White Woods Farm
and nothing said about the children who were alone in the house
and who is it who will give you an hour of earth or a box of forgetting
when all the women want an always and other things that you will never
find in a museum such as the way into another person's dream;
it is after all as the politician said, if you cannot film it nobody wants it
and unless it has been owned by a mystery there is no point in telling us
that the squirrel will be in the Teletower at midnight and other secrets.

And yet, and yet. Here we are at the Pitt Rivers looking into a cask
of invisible years and lost babies and there is a man swallowing Hitler
and a gallery of eyes and if one is brave enough you can listen to the
silences of kings and the drummers in the Barbed Wire Band.

Sudden Light

50th Birthday Poem for Rupert Loydell

The surprise of light opening across fields in late March
when the trees remain solemn and we are still winter people
in our stories and festivals and the gathering of what we have
stored, saved, the density of expectation
and waiting for certain plants and birds and the rising sky
as if certain words were earth and rain
and what we wanted was silent signals and blossom and
corners of the garden to begin rising again
and the knowledge of migrations
as we journey towards wilderness, commitments and commands,
the Easter narrations and what we might take from them
to make our meanings, blindfold beliefs and hide and seeking denials,
what we would place in stained glass, these fracturing epiphanies and
radiant betrayals, our responses to angels and wild words
and the moments of sudden light when stillness pearls
and we settle for the fact that we exist within essential mysteries
and small settlements of faith that will not be defined.
Refusals entice, amazements play games, sacred messages within
skipping songs and radiant riddles and what silence might say.
There, in the square, the deaf violinist knows that we are listening
to what he cannot hear; in his heart he hears it, within his intuition.
By the way; how do you believe in the things you don't believe in
and how does one create a credo of doubt? Sonatas with broken strings.
Meanwhile there are deaf drummers, there are old men hurling themselves
out of aeroplanes, there are blind cyclists, there are bankers who never cheat
at cards, a glassblower in Turin is making the face of Christ out of beer
bottle caps, the blue children on the Isle of Mogh scare the wits out of the
Bishop of Clowwidden when they turn up for Mass, there is nothing more
certain than doubt and he who laughs last should check his fillings.
No journey that is worthy ever quite ends, no long remembered room is
quite as large, the driveway turned left and not right, what the woman
said before she set off to walk the entire coastal path of Britain was try to
remember not to forget.
A knowledge of migrations is always useful; birds, humans, the living and
the dead, silent thunderstorms and the Shirt Museum on the outskirts of
whatsitsname.

What Remains at the Allotments

Sparrow hawk sky and wild bees at nine in the evening
when the last of the light has a drenching exposure
and those still here are carefully placing things in sheds
or stashing what they have grown into the backs of vans
or cars and we are shown the place where a tramp came
to sleep with vagabond dreams and all night I keep seeing
him there and wonder what he did when the vandals came
to smash the greenhouses and spike the pumpkins and did
he want to set his tigers on them and let loose his eagles?
Sometimes the sky is so low it is itself a vegetable and
Doug tells us that you can plant close up to the single hive
and that the wild bees recognise your function and when
the full moon arrives it lifts everything in its tide as if every
window and every door in the world had suddenly opened.

The Cowboys Decide to Leave the Film

The cowboys decide to leave the film
because they have been doing all these things
for years, the same shooting and chasing and always
a backdrop of poor people and ruined churches and
the way their words get mangled by sunsets or winds.
But the horses have to stay. The horses don't know that
there are other places, other ways and so what was left is
a film about horses who continue to move through storms
and amazing sunsets and deserted villages, passing by barns
and ruined farmsteads and empty schoolhouses and locations
where once there were children and old men and women who
for some reason wore waiting like a beautiful dress.
Then, the man who went to the cinema each night of his adult life
walked into the film; we all saw him as he strolled over to one of the
quieter horses and tried to get on. And now he was looking straight at
us as we sat in the cinema and he wanted us to join him and become
cowboys and ride out to shoot the baddies, only we had school the next
day and our parents would never accept what the Manager said.

Snow White and the Silences

In that painting by Paula Rego we see a fat Snow White
with meaty hands and an old woman's knowing eyes
and we wonder what just what she might be thinking
and who kept double-crossing her, who took the chair away,
and when the dwarfs first lied, first spied,
who stuffed nettles in her head, who broke her jokes.
Perhaps none of this happened; perhaps she just got bored by fame
and couldn't find a way out and nobody wanted to know about other
events in her life. Perhaps she has decided to dedicate her life to her
collection of missing things; the one that begins with Red Riding Hood
once she stopped being little and goes on and on and on until we get to
the missing missionaries of Miami. She keeps all this stuff in the cold
basement because warmth would ruin it. There is also a skipping rope
that Stalin used and one of Hitler's dogs and jam jars filled with empty.
In the painting there are other things but it is the eyes that say it all.
These are the eyes of a woman who has seen unicorns on fire, skipped
within a thunderstorm, winked at the tiny faces in the baby tree. These
are the eyes of a woman who has witnessed the bearded Albanian nuns
as they went out each dawn seeking the nests of silver blue unicorns

WHAT ARE THE DEAD FOR?

What are the dead for?
It is to remind us not to hurry.
The poor will give us water
and those who have everything grass.
When we are not thinking the dead
dig themselves up and we can see
how tired the angels really are.
What it is to be entirely alone
in a field and feel the sky suddenly
come down.

The Nuns of Divine Humour

When the nuns were forbidden to play football
or run across the lawns or dip their toes in the lake
or fly kites from the rooftops or whistle like the man
who made ladders and picked their apples and cleaned
the gutters they decided that they should respond with
smiles and winks and wagging fingers and that look that
they remembered their mothers using when what came out
of their father's mouths was piffle and drivel and poppycock;
it was better than silence, it was finer than rules, it was something
that had never been done before; it was better than buns at midnight
or the butcher boy's bum or the music they made with grass blades;
it was more deliberate than a three hour prayer, more complex than
collapsed canticles, more visible than forgetting to believe, more like
wearing a waistcoat of rumours or the burial of very tiny white lies;
so the nuns made a vow and returned to perfect silences, each one,
to protest, to proclaim, to parade and began to grow a ginger beard.

THE POETRY READING AT UNDER ORCHARD MOON

After the three hours of rain we arrived in mud
and the church hall stank of nettles
and there were three nuns in the audience
and Edwardian prints of angels on the walls
and an occasional spider making its seven pm run
and a Muriel Fossett to welcome us and the noise from the pub
was a good idea as we all went across for the local brew
and when we returned to the hall one of the nuns
wanted to tell us about why she was not a boy and the second one
wanted to tell us about Harley Davidsons and we noted her
red rugger socks and the third one beamed and was silent
and it seemed a good idea to read some poems about autumn
and orchards and how to twist the apple free and how at Christmas
a polished apple always fitted the toe of a stocking precisely
and then the bell practice began and it started to rain again
and it seemed a good idea to go back to the pub and its faces
and at closing time the quiet nun wanted to tell us about
writing her poems at three every morning
when she could hardly see the paper to write on
but these ideas had been with her all night like secret stars
and if she did not commit them to paper they might die
like so many things in her previous life in a country that
was no longer on the map and poetry had been banned
and the church bells had all been removed so that they
could no longer remind the people of other things.

Ice Skating at Under Orchard Moon

The vicar is not here. He is uncertain about ice;
what it does to the grimace of the gargoyles,
the way it blinds stained glass, the way that
walking on water now becomes a dare.
Meanwhile the poets are randy for anything
to do with transformations, edges, layers,
the risk of ridicule and redemptions.
And now the mayor has arrived and is attempting
to avoid Mr Lester who wants to remind him of
drownings sixty years ago, as the lake becomes
mosaics, a jazzy infusion, charades and dances
and somebody dressed as a bear keeps toppling
and kids are chasing stars and Lady Stogumber
steps onto the ice as if to demonstrate ballet;her
skirts embracing, her swirls, her girlish giggles,
the lilt of her laughter as if we all have to do
certain things again before we die. To meet our
gentle evasions. Performances against the past.
The vicar is not here. He does not like the swing,
the acrobatic, the way we might become other things
encountering ice, the edge, the massive lift of sky,
and Mr Lester chasing him now with memories
and legends and accounts of a colony of lepers
who inhabited the chapel before the flooding;
the way they huddled and craved and delayed,
the manner of their drowning, searching in the sky
for signs, for messages, from terror into brilliance.

Hurry, Hurry

Hurry, hurry Mister Holy Herbert
hurry down the sun to see the way
a field awakes & all the world stands up
& lupin lights & cartwheeling clouds
& into the church to wake the sleeping bells
& set a rainbow in the soul & find a fox has
been & gone & find his smell like very old;
hurry, hurry for those who are alive must keep alert
& every hedge is thick with hunting creatures
& we must all prepare for bread and blood &
what it is to sing the prayer & whisper bone &
wipe clean the dream to begin again as if this hour
held every life & what we now believe is certain;

for the church is a ship of whispers, a barn of sunrise,
the light leaning across the altar as if to protect, & as
we enter there is that expectation that all may become
changed, the hauling of each hymn & the moment when
a few words reach beyond the mind, the necessary, the now,
& we arrive at a settlement, a place of grace, the intuitive
harmony of what this may be about & its holding us;
the peace that passeth, the peace that is wisdom, the way
that a child discovers things upside down or when there
are voices in the empty field that stop you and there is
no need to reply, the way the final amen is like a long
embrace where there is room for nothing else but love;
& now another day; hurry, hurry, to describe the light;

& listen to the man who has lost his amens
& hear the woman who thinks she is nettles
& see children who are hiding in the mind
& ask teacher who says there are only holes
& tell farmer who keeps his dream in a bucket;
& scold the father with fire in his head and feet
& laugh at the doctor who tells us to clean the grass
& whistle at the verger who says that silence is better;

hurry, hurry Mister Holy Herbert
with hymns in your chest & each day dancing
& the river running sun and stars & what
the words can say may spring surprise & stop us
in a muddle & place a rainbow in our restless lives.

& WHEN IT COMES TO WORDS

& when it comes to words   & when
they may be like kingfishers   & when
or stoats or dragonflies &   like kingfishers
what they do to the heart is   & what they do
make a curious place there   & what they do
so that we all clutch what we so that we all
understand & let it abide   like kingfishers
& it remains with us even   & it remains
into tragedy & betrayals   & it remains
& breaking love & it is   & it remains
the thing that they cannot   it is   the thing
find; the doctor, the parson, it is   the thing
the undertaker, the beloved, or dragonflies
nor earth, rain, flames, charms, or stoats
hymns, letters, diaries, gifts; like kingfishers
gone out, shafts of self &   gone out
what we have made of life   gone out
in silent songs for ever free   in silent   free

like kingfishers

in silent

free

*

Barn

Mrs Harris crosses her heart and puts her summer
into sacks ready to store them in the dry barn.
In winter she wears much the same each day
except on Sunday because of the bells.
Her world is mostly about pigs and chicken and
the way rain has work to do and even the dark of nettles.
She once told the boys that poetry would dry them up
and to put it away until they had nothing else.
After Easter Mrs Harris will take down the sacks
and exchange them. There are only two seasons.
She never looks in the boxes; the boy's diaries,
the drawing books with blue horses and red fields.
There is another barn that she never visits where
she found Mr Harris and the cowman holding hands.

Bound in the Memory of Those Days

Bound in the memory of learning how to cut back, find a line,
clear, slice down, bind and weave, secure the struts again and
make sure it was level and breathing and fit for every season
and wildlife as well as marking boundary, territory, place;

and there was a hedge between the kitchen garden and lawns
where the trades people and servants once walked, out of site
of the rectory drive and the avenue of poplars; boundary,
territory, place, divisions and declarations;

and the ha ha was also a way of controlling the natural landscape
and the cultivated, the croquet lawn and the rose garden and
the remains of an old moat; moorhens, nightingale, owls
and the rooks knowing their place, settlements, positions;

and when the horse died in the glebeland there were six men who
came with ropes and chains to drag it away and they all wore caps,
just like the rat man and the baker and the milkman and the gardener;
uniforms, knowing their place and expectations and rules;

then I went off to boarding school in my first long trousers and
learnt that only the middle button of the blazer must be done up and
walking on the right was essential and the rabbits and owls vanished
and only Mason noticed moths and webs and what moles could do.

A Dream of Elvers

Somerset

The surge of water stroked by moon
and white grass where the green of it had passed
and there was quiet in every field as if we were not
meant to know that they were there in dark millions
and no birds flying and the cows now herded home
and nothing to signal this journeying and impulse and messaging,
these tides of intuition between high banks and silver currents
and the flowing of land and planets and the glass stars
where once men had drowned in their blood with their boys
trying to be soldiers, rebelling, gobbing up ghost grass and mud.

SHIP OF WHISPERS

Sometimes when I enter it is the sound
of things you cannot see that diminishes
the outside world, the obvious, the countless.
Mosaic messages in stained glass, within
wood and the stone cloaks of God's images.
Then a cough disturbs everything or a tourist
who has entered a building but not an abiding
and sometimes there is a child running through
a fountain of light because it is perhaps a toy.
Sometimes also I search for small disturbances;
a bat or a bird or if it is a butterfly I watch as
it searches, seeks, settles for seconds, a bright
restlessness that rises higher and higher until
it has reached a place I cannot see; to die, to
be sublime; to collapse into a dark chancel?
And once or twice there have been others;
men who have come to get warm, hunching
beside radiators, hacking, taking occasional swigs.
And once three clowns came here to be blessed
before the circus set up, leaving leaflets about
acrobats and walking on air and tricks of light
Prayers, parables, the way truths are told and
inside our minds these ornate filters of faith
between what we whisper and what we mean
to believe in fragments of linenfold wisdom.
As the clowns depart I suddenly pray furiously for
Tumbler Tom to cartwheel or flash his blue kazoo.

PISHING

Beneath a yew tree
trying to attract a goldcrest
smaller than a mothball
and listening to the high pitch
and waiting
for it to mistake you
for another bird.

Instead the Rector
asks you to help him
clean up the bat crap
and whilst there you
might also see if
there is any life
in the rat run.

Now that the kites
have returned with their
descanting calls
we spend more time
looking up
aware of these
other territories

and in the church there are
carvings of eagles and herons
and crows and in one window
a lifting of wings in memory of
the kingfisher poet,
his praising pulse,

as if light might be
some kind of love and
birds about returning.

NAMES FOR THE THINGS WE MUST NOT FORGET

The way an evening keeps holding off
and some birds return
to songs

and often it is music waving like a flag
in the head

or the memory of the children telling us
to come as fast as flash because
they had found a dead angel

and when we build the snowman
again we never create the snowwoman
or give her children
or a dog
although nobody has told us not to

and there is that moment at the end
of some films
when each of the actors is seen once again
even the dead ones
even the ones who killed the other ones

as if we should never let go of what we believed
and that there could be other meanings
and every story has
another beginning

if only we gave it time.

THE DREAM DOCTOR TELLS OF THE BLIND OWL

It did not matter at first,
a bird into my dreams, an owl suddenly
entering as if through a window of my mind.

Its light, its caution, its silence holding
my attention beyond calm, and I became
used to its arrival, its place in my world.

Much of my life I have explored such dreams,
brilliant originals, fabulous sequences, the way
we encounter these elements and invasions.

And now I waited, wanted, longed for the owl
to return and I began to understand how it was
held, somehow trapped; that it was blind.

It cannot see me. It cannot consider me wise
lodged between intuition and the invisible
in a smaller world that denies the moon.

I am a voice, a narration, a dream doctor who
catches the signals of stories, these nests in the head,
the sounds of what we hear from what was never said.

And I wonder now if we might exchange something
out of silence and expectation and the way a dream
extends vocabularies and blood knowledge and pulse;

and I want the owl to fly out to see the night trees again
and the way dawn arrives and catch the impulse of this
planet, its awakening and its soundings and abiding eye.

LAPTOP DANCING

It's what you do when there is the beginnings
of a bell in your head and it is too early for wine
and the words click in and out in a sort of tap dance.
It is like sex in that you know it's going on and off
and that you need to go with the bite and the blood
of it now, get it going and out from the heart and save
it for reasons that simply don't feature now. Later
you may remember it, what you meant rather than
what you actually said which is usually where the
dance changes from dancing into the embrace of
other things and the future is remembering already.

Doctor Dunn Has Decided

Doctor Dunn has decided to treat every one
of his patients as if they were a poem.
It is the language that he is interested in
and the run of dialogues and the way some
of the words collect in a phrase that has never
before existed;
such as there is a hole in most of my dreams
and
what does God do in my garden?
and
references to tennis courts and lost pigs
and
the way that angels never stop for windows.
Doctor Dunn does not believe in snow and
sometimes he leaves the television on in case
there are moments of silence
which may quite
terrify.

The Meaning of Light

1.
The man is running out of his house
and all of his family take flight as well
which means the entire idea of family
and trust and books and imagination
and the view from the window and the
sometimes rain and the treasured dreams
and the identity of love and the way the flowers
are arranged and the angle of light in each room
and what the dreams have been delivering and
the language of the eyes and what may be said
at the breakfast table and the conceptions of
what it is that makes each day between ideals
and belief and the idols that we all manufacture.

None of this matters now; the piano is dead,
conversation is an idea, what we said to ourselves
is wallpaper and the possibility of a god has become
a frail fragment of song that is as thin as string and
something to do with what was truth and certainty
and the demise of everything that fell between phrases
and what it might mean and the way poetry betrays as
Lear cowers above his dead daughter and yelps his pain.
None of this matters in the shit of the moment and the
running and the decisions made in seconds as you run out
of the past and every picture you painted and the whiteness
of the future, the unknown textures, the tones that unload in
the soul each mile, each hour, each day and the meaning of light.

Running from what you imagined might be the end of running,
a settlement against truth and fear and what the world might be; and
then the new betrayals of intellect and politics and what the smile
might mean and the way the light in a room portrays the walls and
the ceiling and the floor and the ornaments and everything but the
way of the windows, their view, what they permit, the silences of light
and the declarations of dogma; filth, betrayal, ownership, revenge, and

now you hear the angel speaking in your ear and you do not know if
he is the biggest shit of all, his wings made from the skin of millions
of dead children, his eyes sculptured by screams of the innocent, what he has
to say hacked in a distillation of hell and threnody and the way that
the mad speak in parables when all they want is a silent room and
the sound of grass and the light that sometimes leaps from a distance.

2.

The sound of grass and the light that sometimes leaps from a distance
changes everything when you are high in the sky and taking flight and
towns, tracks, rivers, language, maps change and your hidden possessions
cling between your soul and your ribs and all the time the tribes of your
upbringing clamour in the places where it is safe to stop, when you see
a face in the rain and almost remember a name and when a group of
small children have gathered like gangsters to trick, to trip, their eyes made
of stone or when you are standing in front of a door that will not
be opened and yet you can hear voices from the other side, coughing.
Sometimes sleeping in a tree would be good; better than huddling in
a hedge. Sometimes the rain racing towards you enters the head and
you know that you are drowning. Sometimes it is like lying beneath
snow and you can hear wild animals and you dare not eat the snow.
You have already devoured roots and berries and sucked grass and
thought about eating a dog, if you could catch it and kill it and keep it
down. Keep it and other things down. Keep the elements down. Earth.

3.

Sometimes when I was thinking about the paintings that I must create,
that would come from me, that were my testimony, I knew that the
people would be flying across the landscape, the towns, the villages, the holy
places, the fields. But they would not be in dreams; they would be actual.
They would be the identity of the pictures. They would be the stories and
the sounds and story tellers. How can you have this? How

can they become in the sky? How can we believe in them above the ground as if there is another place to be alive? How can we accept this?
Easily. It is so simple. So there is a wife and a child and a bride and birds and musicians and whatever they may mean. Easily. So here is what they are wearing and looking like and even what they are saying. Easily. You just have to keep your own two feet on the ground and look above and greet them. You do this every time you pray. You do this every time you praise. You do this when you are in love and when you want to be in love. You do this when you think about the dead and where you shelter them now in your living ways. To see them. To hear them. To listen to them. Sometimes you answer back. You do this at certain festivals and when there are bells ringing and when there is some dancing and men who can be so quiet break into song or begin juggling and when the teacher has given up dates and numbers and begins to tell you a wonder. And you then realise that the things above your head also have their seasons of light and meaning and atonements.

Little Banjos

for Christopher Middleton

He plays the piano in his sleep,
the piano plays the sleep in him;

he places chairs in the garden,
the garden places chairs in him;

once more the sun umbrella rises
and each day provides its little banjos.

And it is now, this moment, when he knows
that he will propose marriage to her;

they are both aged 83 and they marry;
and she dances for him and she dies.

The next day he plays the piano and sees her
in the sky and the piano music smells of grass

ON THE SEVENTH DAY

He has been inside the earth for six days now.
Tomorrow she will visit him to talk about
what she has done with the letters, the diaries,
the box of old photographs, postcards and their noises,
the three wristwatches that haven't worked for years,
the return of foxes.

On the seventh day she will wait until evening
and then walk into the garden, still hearing voices,
and talk about what she has been saying to God;
she will then return to the silence of the house;
later, in the bedroom, in that enormous flood,
her arms will be filled with garlands of stars.

STEALING THUNDER

The door to the house belongs to the garden
the garden belongs to the stone wall
the stone wall belongs to the hill
the hill belongs to the crags
the crags belong to Italy
to the ideas in the minds of old men
as they sit at the back of the cafés
with their glasses half filled with wine
half filled with stars
and they think of what life has been
and what they must leave behind
which will be two shirts
and three songs
and a view of the hill at dawn
that brings them to their senses
and what they never said
to the sons who have vanished
and the waiting daughters.

A Whistling Woman

A whistling woman does not let the trees
grow under her feet and knows the names
of the woods where each boy lies.

A whistling woman reaches for the tallest stories
and lets a silent room hide its secrets
even when the sun sits down.

A whistling woman will tell you about islands
in the mind where the noise of the geese
tells the farmers to close their fields

and that a man comes each day to tell them
that they have no letters or parcels to receive
and that the wind has hidden their words.

A whistling woman lays out a meal for two
and as she pours a glass of milk she says
the same name over and over and over

as if she were stitching a quilt of whispers.

Improvisations and Improvements

Pablo Casals

Aged 93 he continued to practice for three hours a day
certain that he was improving and that some moments
were more radiant than others, more becoming wonder;

and the man who changes lightbulbs on the Eiffel Tower
knows that he has been in the sky all day and yet he is
still human, a man with a wife who sometimes snores;

and Fat Fred Fielding, when he does his thing with the empty
paper bag remembers his dad teaching him this trick and telling
him to look out for the way some women take off their shoes

at the end of a day and sometimes when they lay the tablecloth
it is more like a scene in a painting where the light arrives
from some corner of the mind and you can hear it, entering.

Fox Unknown

Fox unknown in the traces of the deep
the voices unheard or the silence as a code
as beneath the sun and moon we survive

the river rising deep in memory or loss
and between wars and memory we tell
each other what we want to hear

until a clown or a child tumble a new truth
and the fox ambles towards what the woman
provides and the sun sets out its sunsets

that will do for awhile as the angels gather
with snow dream flowers that grow in the head
and what the dead left unsaid.

Momentous Explorations of Faith

There are moments when this world is grass
and we invent memories to accompany dreams
and writing another fiction is a way of keeping
the clown at bay and the stillness of our parents
and the recognition of things before they begin.

Every tradition is new and what was linen fold
becomes a straight line and what is not actually
here hides just behind the last moment ready to
say boo and codswallop and even the preacher
reaching the climax has other things in his head.

What appeared to be a miracle was a mixture of
bad light and a tricky wind, the dancers know that
it will all end in rain and when the hot air balloon
lands at the old people's home it is filled with more
mumbo jumbo and books about life before birth.

When will it all begin and who will remember to
feed the dancing bear once we have all said hey ho
and will there still be baked beans for tea and those
small coughs before a prayer begins and what I wanted
to ask the bishop was when did he begin to shave his legs?

At the convention of clowns there is a moment when
they all try to make themselves invisible and it always
works and there is applause and marks are awarded and
the reality is that not one of them can see whether they are
there at the time or not and they never wish to admit it.

A Short Guide

Be brief and keep it simple, otherwise they will start telling you
about themselves and other houses they have visited and making
improbable connections relating to names of towns and rivers and
other transformations.
Be sure that they purchase a Guide Book; refer to specific pages and
let them do the work pertaining to pictures and events and the way that
the places at the table are set out.
Never let them sit down but do if any one of them is capable get them
to play the piano.
The things that will catch their attention are photographs of the living,
the several bathrooms, modern books in the library, images of the garden
in times past and of course infidelities. Do not answer any questions
about the latter. As they get to the end focus on the tea room and small shop.
They will of course stare at all the PRIVATE notices, the DO NOT ENTER
signs, praying for a notable person to step out.
Never mention the ghosts, the missing child, the court case because they
are perfectly capable of making these up as they go along.
Do not be surprised if they linger at the Ha Ha, staring across at the
cows or at the fallen trees as if they owned the place.
Only a few will notice the photographs of those who went to the wars.

A Snowman

I am out here making some noise
and they have put all the trees away.

They have put all the trees away and
I am out here making some noise in
a way that you may want me to hide.

Sometimes they do not let the words out
in case they say things that have never been
and this can be a great concern to the trees

so they put the trees away and the windows
continue to weep and when I reach the top
of the field there will be a snowman to tell.

The Colours of Music

Sometimes our children dream so hard
they find other lives in tangled light
and suddenly wake up to love us again;

they invent names for animals we never see
and other children who wait for them
and suddenly wake up to love us again;

when they are older they will put away such
adventures and find a name for everything
and silently decide to love us again;

sometimes a riddle or the colours of music
will remind them or a sudden dragonfly
catching light as it flees from rain;

or when we explore the photo album
and they see their secrets now exposed
and wake up to forgive us again.

The Mothers of Plaza de Mayo

The mothers of Plaza de Mayo no longer believe in dawns
even a glass of water looks different and the taste of bread
and wild grass will cover everything including dreams.

What are the dreams for? What is the point of blue?
The door lets nothing in and each room is about things
that cannot be said without the sensation of burning.

There used to be songs and between the dances jokes
and the way a child went up to a horse ready to tell
about names and the stories of their lives.

Sometimes at the meal table we know that they are here;
dead or alive they have come back and sit down with us;
silence of a spoon, the way the sliced pear shines.

Each night their bed is ready in a room filled with moon.
There will be time to embrace the body, read the letter,
talk to the child who will never arrive.

In Praise of Older Trees

The way a day enters without words,
out of a dark now;
thousands of seasons and reformations
constantly cascading,
earthing beyond colours and wonder,
surviving beyond our recognition
so that very young children dream them
as if they were rope tricks or kite catchers,
or castles for birds or something coming
out of an ancient skyburst
and we know that they might outlive
our reasoning and portrayals
and the stories we keep for the unborn;
the yes of the ancient and the whispers
of now and the way a bough hides millions
and garlands of stars as we enter dawns
and mornings and stories of afternoons
and each person carries a sense of secret
creatures who once made us aware of our
place on this planet, the orderings of the
extraordinary, the way we eat water and light.

Earth Works

1

Early morning, as if it has been raining
so that the ground rises to meet the sky
and we know that we cannot be alone.
Where there were stars the trees strain
and there are so few people awake each
one makes a story of faith and endeavour
and the slow persistence of earth songs.
Always birds and the low percussion of
cars and letterbox yawping and then the
radio voice telling us nothing has changed
between our sleep and what the world has
been doing and weather reports as if we are
ruled by rains and wind and distant mists.
Is it because we live on an island that clouds
and clocks, coasts and rivers stay in our hearts
and why we seek sunsets as nature's amens?
And we keep writing about the dead as if it
is this that stops them knocking at our door,
our hide and seeking natures at work in every
story and stained glass window as if anything
might vanish, might change forever, never was.

2

The three horses appear on the snowy field,
quiet as grass, as stone. They cautiously explore
the high field and come down to the freezing stream.
This is where my father stood blessing the field in spring,
the farmer with his heavy amens and his son in a wheel chair
who saw sun and sensed winds and tall trees that held up the light
of his days, the sound of his being, the sight of what was,
each word that might create a statement, a call to knowing.

The mother said nothing as the horses came close and the two men broke into another hymn. And now it is a flat land, the low sky laden, waiting for rooks. The digging deep into anything that will take them through this winter with the wife gone and the boy wanting stories and the house made if ice.

My Life as a Handbag

It was meant to be about discovering the way
normal things have a life of their own in order
to protect them from the autonomy of boredom;
at least that was the pretext and the big idea was
to be the exposure of small events in the life of
closed cafes, ironed shirts, dead sheds, the falling
vase. And that was it until the vase actually fell
and the small dog bit the postwoman and the man
on the radio had a coughing fit and the glass danced
everywhere leaving a unique pattern and some of it
got into the handbag which got this off in the first place,
which means that what might come last could be counted
first and didn't Salvador Dalí work up some of his shapes
with matchstick men and all the time we are working our
way through space and what is not imagined does not exist
and a very small part of the soul can suddenly become the
opening line of a poem about discovery and the way light
enters the head and a field of wheat can recover from thunder
although the children have all run into other lives and keep
skipping from one story to another to make it more like
real life where vases fall and voices are raised and what we
say sometimes comes out as if somebody had cut the strings?

Ice Man

I am out here making some noise. You can say what you like
but I will not hear you. The garden is nowhere to be seen as it
has snowed for three weeks and the weeping windows see nothing.

I have not written any letters for years. It is best like this for the
postman has not been here at all and I can hardly remember where
it was that I buried the telephone. Perhaps it was in another.

The vicar used to call but now he has better things to do with God
and he will never know that I still hum the hymns, the old ones that
provided a radiance and made you think there was something more.

I am out here making some noise. When they discover me there
will be nobody to inform. I have begun to smell like nettles in this deep.
The doorbell won't tell a thing and there isn't a cat.

The lake maps me and those cold corners of stone and the
gobs of gargoyles. I keep away from angels who might still
clasp sun. Sometimes I grip grass so hard I can hear it whinge.

Ghost Dancing Etc

We were meant to join the others in the apple orchard.
It seemed that we had been doing this for years and the blossoming
and fruiting and bringing out the ladders and being told to twist
and not pick and how to prevent bruising had become more ritual than
adventure and fresh air and chatting up the women and getting away
from the wards and the television talk and the rustling of flesh.

It was Jack who was first, taking a left instead of a right and then Ralph and
Richard and then Ben who always looked as if he had just seen an
angel or Jesus or both. And nobody noticed because of the sun and the
way the days drifted after lunch and some of the nurses sunbathed and
anyway the Big Beast was away for a week with Mrs Beast and brats.
So we all took a left and headed off for the park and the lake etc.

It was OK until we got to the etc. The park was packed and nobody took
any notice of Ben even when he peed in a bush but when we saw
the ice cream van there was a problem because we didn't do money
anymore;bit like The Queen. So Jack told the bloke to put it on the tab
and he told Jack it wasn't a pub and then this man in a suit came up and
said he would treat us all as Ralph looked like his old man. Five 99s.

After that we wandered into the town and into Tesco and nobody took any
notice. The loos were nice and we helped ourselves to the soap bars and then
we found the tea room and ordered a slap up feast and
one by one we made it out via the toilet at the back and into the car park
and when we thought it was about time we headed back but Jack had taken
a right instead of a left and one by one we all did the same.

They found Ben in a church and Jack in a pub and Ralph in a tree
and Richard had got onto a train going to somewhere or nowhere.
Meanwhile I was everywhere;cleaning windows, opening doors,
selling the flowers I snatched from graveyards, collecting coins from phone
boxes, helping myself to milk bottles and every night I climbed
into the stained glass window in the church and became a Green Man.

We Are All Living in the Piano

The hedges were stripped already; the ditch diggers
had long gone and then these machines came plunging
and ripping and water and wildlife deserted.
When they came for the trees they said they were
looking for trees that would make millions of matchsticks
and we were amazed by the arithmetic of this and the cash.
Then came Gardens Tax, Tall Tree Tax, Lawn Tax, Roses Tax
and fields became fables, the lost kingdoms of woods and glebeland
and grass was poetry and rural was cut glass.
What mean moat? What mean byre? What mean elver?
There were some who protested from trees and tunnels
and thousands who stood on the beaches belching Blake
and the suicides of so many children.
Now we hide in grandfather clocks and what remains of churches
and deserted cinemas and a few have taken to hiding beneath war
memorials and village halls and wrecked caravans and grand pianos.

Where the Sea and the Sky Seem to Meet

You can look out and not be sure where sea ends
and sky begins. It appears to change all the time
and there is something of glass, of mirror about it
as if there is something there we are not meant to
make out and understand. It can happen with fields
as well and sometimes in the moments when an
afternoon is becoming evening and one looks at
a line of trees and the sky holds onto them or they
hold up the sky. I suppose some of the poets have
written of this and the man in the village who says
he carries such things into songs but I never get
to hear his music on the radio. On the radio they
have a lot of this seeing and not seeing because
they leave you to work on it in your own head;
what you see in a lane, what trees say, what the
wind is doing and what horses make of it all.
And then the pigs. Such great lumbering things
in a world of mud and muck and when they lie
down they almost fold over on each other and
you can imagine what they are thinking about
is to do with the next feed. There used to be a
man who took them onto the beach and ran them
to the edge of the sea to clean them. They didn't
seem to mind it until men on horses came along
and the pigs made up their mind pretty quick and
were off back up the beach and into the lane. Then
the horses would stand still for a long while as if
they were comfortable by the movement of the sea,
its silver and its shapes and the way it had sound
that was not like anything else; not rainfall, not lake,
not like the dark river. The horses and the noises
they made standing there and far far out the sea
and the sky meeting and the men on the horses.

SOMETIMES

Sometimes, on Dartmoor, in early autumn,
you will see pairs of shoes set carefully by the roadside.
It's where ramblers have changed into boots, built up shoes,
ready for any sudden change of weather or land loss, the way
what was mapped can flash into the unknown.

Today, heading south, we wonder what would happen if shoes
were still there at seven in the evening, unclaimed.
The sheep don't seem to see them in the fine glow of rain
as they wait for ancient silence and green sleep.

Later, coming back from Plymouth, we see the shoes
have gone, nobody will be called out to search;
and then one of the children spies something between stubborn
tufts of grass and we stop the car and walk back to find a pair
of child's ballet shoes.

FEAR OF CLOWNS

After the Circus Master's bow and the lights dimming
and an end to the music, father took us behind the scenes,
insisting that we needed autographs or to see the horses;

and there was nobody there, the magic had been packed,
they had all gone to their caravans or out to a meal, into
the rain and the town or to hide their secrets in silence;

and the cages were dark and hard until we found the circle
of clowns, talking in a prayer about what they feared, as if
they too were animals, tricksters, trained, bandits of magic;

and the one who came over to us to tell us that we should not
be there was about as tall as I was, I could smell his nettles,
I could see the face behind the paint beyond his mask of lies;

and I wondered about the deaths of clowns and did the mask
come off, did others see the real face as they prepared him for
the big event, the final disturbance of fire or earth or stars?

WE DO THINGS

For Kier and Danny

I have just been taught by my grandson how to armfart.
We do things like this between cheating at croquet and
wondering how many birds it takes to fill a tree at night.
We also know about blowing on grassblades stretched
tight between our thumbs and how to open umbrellas
inside a car and the essential difference between eating
three pancakes and four on a Sunday before the church
thing with its noises and silences and the way the organ
can raise everything up so that nothing else gets in much.
The younger grandson observes all this and will probably
be a good whistler. When we said goodbye to the very old
lady today he was worried because she is so lonely. If she
is so sad and lonely, he said, why doesn't she have a baby?

PART TWO

The Owl Wife Speaks

1.

But she does not, she does not.

What is it that night tells
that he cannot?

Is it about other, some things
else, altering stories

or perhaps the colours of dark,
the seeking silences.

When she returns, drenched,
words do not come;

no knowledge or suspicion
or whisper

as she slides into a bed
that no longer travels,

and she will say nothing
between the ceiling
and his shoes

and the knowledge of a field.

2.

When he has gone out
silence is a drift
of regret.

His odour still pauses
and what might have

been said
stands naked by the
watching window

as she carefully
arranges ideas
for the day

and what she must do
with hours and abidings
and the preparation
of small sentences

as if
their marriage
might be a
fragment
of forgettings.

3

Water is the wine of time
as it clothes
the closeness
of her nakedness
and balms

but downstairs
the frantic silence
and what love
is this
untidy
solitude,

this empty
kettle,
dirty
plate,
cold
seat,
dry
closing?

4.

Perhaps he will never return
and the accident that takes him
will heal every future hour

and she will learn to fly again
and become the sky again
and find another
tree

and nest.

5.

Meanwhile
the knowledge
of a field;

wind knowledge
and barbed wire
and nothing gate
and bark beginning
over and over
as if God did not care
the mirror moon

and the owls
about her body
and the flying
and the way
she speaks
to their necessity
again again again.

6.

She might write winds
she might dance rain
she might whistle sorrow
she might sew wounds
the glass of her blood
always still.

7.

When he talks to the horse
he does not use words;

head down into the nettle light the fields folding
and everything he sees an event that he cannot stop;

even the pigs know what they must do and these walls
have winds and tracks fall back onto the stones of memory;

within his father's kingdom he is lost, the one who remained,
planting in the same places, the orchard heavy with voices;

when he talks to the horse the lichen silence moulds maps
and the sky comes closer to tell its stories.

8.

She does not write her story
in and out of the hours when he is away and lost
and the small rooms play their games
to remind her of the lost children and the hidden toys
and the way earth betrayed them all and the stubborn
stay stay stay that has become a statement of stones and
a stale ritual and it is only the owls that she might inform
and she would speak about the fall of each season and what
was rose time and winter song and how days became heavy pages
in a book she never read and how he spent more time with the outside
and she knew he could no longer enter her and the bed
        became another
silence, silence, silence as if there were snow there and ancient darkness
and slate dreams and rumours and small anecdotes of derision falling.

9.

She does not know why she returns

the owls have nothing to say

the night hides everything

her being there becomes its own territory

as if no other place might let her in

as if she might never leave here

and the man never discover her again.

ENTERING LIGHT AT ST IVES

1.

Silence becoming light silence,
stone becoming the speech of light.

2.

Entering light that lifts
and what the mind will make of this
and what cannot be said cascading
into something only attempted.

3.

What we bring here falls back
because of perceptions and expectations
and what the mind insists upon.

4.

What the sea says when it meets the sky,
what the water makes of tides and time
and the gorse garlanding.

5.

I came here to be with others
and as I entered I was alone again
sand into sky into sun.

6.

The words on the grave tiles muttering
but I could not hear them because
of the words held in my heart.

7.

The light says yes and the silence says
listen to me and the music says if only
we had more time.

8.

What do we bring but the noises that have failed us?
What do we ever say but other people's riddles?
These stones reaching above our definitions of eternity.

9.

And is the God here, intent, listening?
Does He see us in our hauling of the holy,
does He care about our futures and fumbling,
does he go out into the shades of trees and listen
as our silences begin again, as we walk away and
drive back to our houses and careful constructions?

10.

The centre of the stone is moon,
in the healing, in the shaping, in the way of the idea;
the centre of the wood is winds,
in the holding form, in the seeking, in the branching of it;
the centre of the light
coming out of winter fields and walls that have lost their place
and ancient villages that have returned to earth.

11.

At Easter, on the seeking shore,
those with necessary prayers
and bells in the head,
pilgrims seeking
their child of light.

SAINT FRANCIS AND THE DEATHS

And they bring more dead birds to Saint Francis
who lays them in a circle on the ground
so that at dawn perfect light will discover them
and they will ascend again.

And now they carry a dead fox to him
and he responds with a slow dance
and then he begins clapping his hands
and calling to the dead creature;

"Fox, fox, come out of death and be born
for today there will be sun and wind and later
the sky will dance with stars
as if for the first time."

And the man with no hands
commences clapping
in his head.

Saint Francis Went Out into the Snow

Saint Francis went out into the snow
clothed only in the light of stars
because the flowers do not wear clothes
and the poor have no garments
and those who have lost their minds
wear only madness
and the dead
are clothed in grass.

Saint Francis and the Bells

Saint Francis understood what the bells were saying
but not the drums.
The bells summoned, proclaimed, said it was time
to pray, lifted the dead to radiance.
The drums took young boys to be soldiers
and gave the condemned no hope
and roared into dreams of beasts and demons.
Saint Francis blessed the bells
but when he stared into the eyes of the drummer boys
he saw vultures in their eyes
and their mothers harvesting stones.

SAINT FRANCIS AND THE FLYING FATHER

She told Saint Francis
how she kept seeing her father flying in the sky;
he had his working clothes on and seemed always
to be in such a hurry. Did Saint Francis know what
it might mean?

"Your father is not here. What you see comes from
your mind. It is about something unfinished perhaps
or the chains of your love. When you next see him up
there wave to him and offer him a glass of water and
invite him to sit in your garden.
That will do it.
Don't send him away."

And once or twice before his death
Saint Francis looked up
and saw two figures
moving across the summer sky.

SAINT FRANCIS AND THE CONFUSIONS OF FAITH

Sometimes there were tides in his mind
drowning what he knew and understood
and even the wisdom of the horses.

It was then that the Man of Sorrows came again
with his stone stories and promises of healing
and when he arrived the river ran wild.

Saint Francis wished that he could tell his father
about giving everything away, even the things that
you did not have but sometimes forgiveness was like
an inquisition, a disbelief in belief.

And the dreams were never of any use; the dreams never
ended and never began and when he broke into a run
the three horses belonging to his neighbour
didn't even look up.

So he ate flowers and healed pigs and made the lepers laugh
and taught the children how to listen to a field and told the very
old women that there was a marvel waiting for each of them and
that poverty was about simplicity
and how they should look out for
the madness of kings.

SAINT FRANCIS AND THE LAST SONGS

Saint Francis listened then to the last songs;
birds, young mothers, a group of children, some
people burying their dead.
There were these moments when sounds became stories,
mosaics of meaning and taut transparencies
before the low call of the evening
as each tree cools and small terraces flicker light
and the movement of horses
returning from necessary journeys.

The Gifts of Saint Francis

I will give you even what I do not own;
the silence of the sun on grass,
the way the earth returns,
the knowledge of the tree,
the calm of the horses early in the evening,
the history of a stone,
the solitude of a lost day,
the vision of the song bird,
the last sight of the first home,
the comfort of the chair,
the blind child's dance,
the unsaid prayer.

PART 3

The Bible in the Fridge

Who put the Bible in the fridge?
Was it to make it more elemental
or more of a warning?
Was it because I would need fire
to bring it back to life
or would hugging do the trick?
I had once seen a man hugging at tree
in the hospital grounds and he looked
ecstatic with his clothes placed
in a neat little bundle on the ground.
The Bible took up very little space
between the bottle of white wine
and the half loaf of wheatgrain
as if somebody might soon come
back for the comfort of it.

On the Stairs

And it is nearly always on the stairs, coming down
to see if the post has arrived, or at night when the alarm
has been set and you carry a book or a magazine and you
hope that there will be no more telephone calls today.

Sometimes it is mother, years ago, asking you if you have
done something, or the child calling, or you meet yourself
carrying a suitcase. Sometimes it is something actually
there, on the stairs. Mostly it is about something that has
to return, to be completed, in your or someone else's head.

Afterwards, briefly, it turns in your mind or curls into
the next dream, or you write it down as I am doing now.

ON THE FIRST DAY

for Asher and Emily and Prev

You have heard your mother's voice so many times
and now you can feel how she belongs and taste her,
and here is warm, cold, being lifted, kiss and the coiling
of other voices, the chimes of noise, as you enter world;
and we have been waiting and sending messages and
hearing your signals, your journey, and what was so long
a waiting becomes sudden; every hour newness, every day
exploration and response and trusting what you cannot yet
see; and on the first day we celebrate, we name, we describe,
and what we are doing is loving, is making a picture that will
surround you and grow larger and gradually make a tapestry
of faces, songs, stories, laughter, the sun and moon welcoming.

POEM

Here is a room and people will come in
and make their days in the same way they
enter ideas and make up stories and some
even wish they might write an entire book.

They do not do this with dreams because
the dream is a creature itself and there will
be things quite beyond like discovering the
mystery in the tree is an angel that was not

meant to be there or the man who is lifted
away by the kite had wanted this to happen
all of his fidgety life and anyway nobody
can trust a dream in the way they let music

into the deepest part of their ideal meaning;
so this poem is really about what we are able
to do with words and kindnesses and the way
we sometimes see things just before they are.

Old Man in a Field

A field is always filling, even when
you walk there alone;
earth knowledge and ancient rain
and things as yet not gathered in.

A gale knows this as it strips to stone
and the staggering sun in late February;
at Easter hedges and walls begin to rise
and you can see the past as mosaics.

And now it is you, old man in a field,
wishing that you could jump a cowpat
or see the world as a bird from a tree,
waiting for things to happen, arrivals;

ready to open a gate
that only you can see.

NOWHERE

The beautiful dead don't have wings; they have
no need to travel now; they can visit the places
they always wanted to without flying, and there
are times when they simply want to rest in places
they once loved and hear the trees again and the
way water talks, especially after all night rain;
they may even want to enter a café and see
what it means now that they have given up food
and they watch the way that wine comforts and
of course there is some wallpaper music; why did
it mean so much, why did it make all the difference
to a conversation, was it about avoiding silence
which was sometimes essential in a church or when
a man comes back from his drowning and you do
not greet him because he is not there; the dead know
about such things, how beginnings and endings are
part of the same story, how finally there is nowhere.

My Grandmother Entering Heaven

It looks as if she is swimming through the silver bits
because her dress is so huge and she always carries an umbrella
and the handbag still holds her personal things.

What will the gardeners do and her son who will weep for weeks
and does she still smell of mints?

Of course she knows what to expect; most of her life has been a preparation
and the fact that there is nobody else around just goes to prove something
she learnt in a sermon years ago.

What will the servants say and who is going to give the children chocolate
and does she need shoes?

In her garden the tulips crack and collapse and the letter she was composing
finishes itself.

Molly Warding Off

Elaine Pamphilon

Then there come these days when what you would wish for
slides away into another life; some other space that may not in
fact exist; but then that is so with many of our hours and ways.

So here is Molly warding off the pigeons again so that they
will not wreck her small kitchen garden and she will be able
to listen to gulls and wait for the dolphins and puffins.

There are ten pigeons strutting about on the red kitchen roof
and the cat has quite given up was Molly waves her violin,
tapping the strings ready to attack with a blast of Mozart.

But there are several ways of seeing things; the pigeons gather
because they adore the way Molly plays, she entices them with
the bow, the cat is deaf, the tender plants shoot up.

Sara from next door will soon arrive with her father's trombone
and the vicar's sister with one of those portable organs; to make
winter wait, to ward off certain silences and faces in the rain.

MISTER CLOUD SAYING FAREWELL

Mister Cloud is saying farewell to Garland Rock
and all that is not there, forgiving clockwork dreams
and hats in the garden and the way that letters never;

coming across the shopping list but now they are closed
and the way the church bell was like a bandit and what
took place when all the taps were turned on in summer;

and what was sometimes said was weather and where do
we appear on the map and if we are not living sideways
what is the point of gulls over the bay and winter moon?

Mother said once was enough and when she heard rain
in her head she ran so fast the light went out and we were
left with washing up and dead socks and the geese to feed;

father said it would all become true at church so we sang
the holy and prayed the singing and shook hands with silence
and the orchard became a place where sun could cut you;

sometimes I am coming there again and the memories skip
on the lawn and I can hear the darkness of the barn and see
Ann Craze with wind in her knickers standing upsidedown.

MEMORY

Memory is often about forgetting;
most of all it is about what did not happen
in a classroom, a silent room, a field;
the way we weren't.
Father was sometimes grass and mother
skipping rope and trees wore clouds as if
they cared.
Once we saw mother whispering what might
have been a prayer as she lowered three kittens
into a bucket.
The postman delivered rain again
and once in Cornwall we saw a man
in a pram.
And now I expect memory will more and more
become what we tell our children
about sunsets and the gaps in the photograph album
and why you have to be careful with stories about owls.

It Will Be Better Yesterday

The way that words can garland
what we have failed to understand
because we are so quick, so now, so urgent.
Is it uncertainty again almost thrusting away
as if knowledge might invade and persuasions
of yesterday, like good bread or the silence
of apples or a third glass of wine?
Why do I keep hearing my father humming carols
or see the red setter racing waves at low tide
and what is the point of all these books and papers and
who needs old diaries and family Bibles?
Late November; the holly berries about to be taken and
each day I check the temperature in New York.
Advent with its slow motion and ways of discovering us;
birth lights, sudden stars, our gardens hide and seeking
beneath a waiting moon.

I've Been Here to Tell You

I've been here to tell you
I'm not here anymore.
I can do that now.

The door to the summerhouse
sometimes lets you know
that no day is the same.

Even old songs tell us this
and the way a prayer always
takes a new direction.

This August summer escaped
and green children hugged
the density of hedgerows.

At the windfarm we saw
angels cartwheeling and
heard their timbrels.

The way a field never closes
and can you see yourself
between the kite and sun?

I Think We Could Be Very Happy Here Until We Aren't

All adventures of the heart start this way,
the delightful dins of love;
every window giving us full moons,
old men coming up with that sort of a wink
and flower sellers dropping the price
as a smart investment
and even the park manager invites us onto the grass
telling us the names of trees and birds and about the
celebrities who wrote verse here or danced by the lake.

Much later white grass decides to grow across the mirror
and cobwebs seem to clap their hands just out of reach
and the place where the spilling coffee dug a hole in the
fitted carpet waits for you to move house before it exposes
and you keep seeing the place where Old Custer did his
last wag and the children ran in and didn't understand.

Of course there is nothing original about any of this;
we don't do murders, we never wanted one of those
dwarf pigs and when we downsize we will
pack our secrets in glass apartments
and discover a few objects that we thought we had
given to the church and there will be fights about books.

Why is it that so many books belong to our lives
and so many of them stay asleep now
like old toys and even old jokes
and the punch lines have grown new skins?
Church bells remain the same and photographs
of New York and the sun getting up to dress
and that image of a man in a pram chewing his cigar
and once I remember seeing a chap cycling across
the sunset at Padstow and knowing it was Malcolm Arnold.

Broken Things

The voice from the father marching behind closed doors
with bits or radio butting in and even some music
and then the lowering tones before the silence
as if a tiger had entered the room or a dead uncle
in a large photograph has stuck out his tongue.

The voice of the mother somewhere attempting to tame
and her face, her hands, her small persuasions helpless
and lost as the voice of the father bangs on and becomes
short bursts and you know that it will run down and
drain and that sentences will strangle themselves.

The music is turned up. A door bangs. The grandfather
clock sends its message about time and night and what
we all have to learn and the entire house seems to be
listening, waiting, yearning. Somebody is coming upstairs.

Abbotsfield Farm

The boys are up at Berry Rise searching for Harley Davidsons.
They criss-cross the field with their metal detectors each Easter
week seeking resurrection stories, something wonderful to make
them famous in the village. Sod history; heigh ho the Harleys.
One boy drinks cold tea, the wiser one chews gum, makes notes.
Buds are breaking now, shoots and shots of green. Earth rising.
The smell of a badger. From here you can see the edge of Devon,
the wide bay, small farms, wind warped hedges and the squat
tower of St Ennis. Sometimes something signals; spades, fencing,
chains, trash. They never talk about the Harleys, the way they might
be tight in sheeting, wound in whispers and gossip tangled in rumour.
From here they can see their own place; the barn, the long low roof.
They can see dogs in the yard waiting for rats and sometimes the
old woman in the orchard wrestling with shirts and sheets. They can
hear the bang of the tractor starting its roar. They can sense a fragile
tapestry. Sometimes it looks like another world, it has other smells.
Some days they want never to return, to find coins, goblets, things the
abbots hoarded and become famous in the bay. They can see the school
bus with its skinny kids and the fat twins and when the church clock
strikes they run back for the milking, the churning cow noise, the voice
of the old man as he bullies them and accuses them and lunges with
words. Later they gob grubb letting the cider seize them, the television
winks its images telling them about other people, what the world is up
to, the weather man presenting thunder and rain as if he ran the show; a
detective sucking his pipe as he strings out the suspense, images of men
dressed in blood and the blah blah blah of some priest telling them it is
a special time, that there is more to life than death, that there are many
rooms and mansions and what to say if we are chosen. Christ's army.
One of the dogs brings in a dead owl. The generator fails again. Rain
runs into their dreams. One boy digs up the remains of a woman who
looks as if she is silver and could come back and might have wings.
His brother lifts up the head of a baby. Sod rain. Sod the living dead.

Lightning Source UK Ltd.
Milton Keynes UK
174319UK00001B/5/P